ULTIMATE
QUESTIONS &ANSWERS
HISTORY
AND CULTURE

AUTUMN
PUBLISHING

CONTENTS

THE BEGINNING OF CIVILIZATION...4

RELIGION AND CULTURE...14

ANCIENT HISTORY...................................32

MODERN SOCIETY...................................48

WHEN DID THE FIRST HUMANS LIVE?

Although humanlike creatures have existed for millions of years, the first civilised humans appeared about 300,000 years ago. The earlier creatures, called hominins, were of many different kinds. They were more like apes, with long arms and big jaws. Gradually, over time, they evolved and became more and more human.

The apelike hominin

WHO WERE THE NEANDERTHALS?

Humans belong to a group of mammals called *Homo sapiens.* The term means "wise man." Appearing about 120,000 years ago, Neanderthals were the first species of *Homo sapiens.* They had a bigger brain than their ancestors, and a strong muscular body. It is not yet known why Neanderthals became extinct.

Portraying a Neanderthal making fire

Big ?

WHO WERE THE FIRST HOMININS?

Hominins, called *Australopithecus,* existed around four million years ago in Africa. *Australopithecus* means "southern ape," and they were an intermediate species between apes and humans. Like humans, most southern apes walked upright and were just over three-feet tall. They had a small brain, an apelike jaw and a hairy body. They lived on fruit and vegetables. Hominins began to spread out farther, to other continents, about two million years ago.

Australopithecus

WHO WAS LUCY?

In 1974, paleoanthropologists—scientists who study hominin fossils—Donald Johanson and Tom Gray found the partial skeleton of the earliest known hominin at that time, in Hadar, Ethiopia. They named her Lucy. By studying Lucy, they found that upright walking evolved long before hominins began using stone tools, and also before their brains began to expand. Lucy lived 3.2 million years ago.

The fossilized, partial skeleton named "Lucy"

WHO WERE THE FIRST HUNTERS?

Homo erectus

The earliest hominins were primarily vegetarians, like apes. About 1.5–2 million years ago, *Homo erectus,* meaning "upright man," appeared. This species began hunting and eating meat. They could light fires, cook food, and hunt with wooden spears.

Homo erectus was the first species to spread across Africa—their remains have been found as far away as Russia and Indonesia.

WHEN WERE TOOLS USED FOR THE FIRST TIME?

Though there is evidence of crude tools being used much earlier, it was about two million years ago that the hominin *Homo habilis* or "handy man" used tools with skill. *Homo habilis* lived in Africa. He had a large brain and used tools to cut hides to make clothes, and chop food for eating.

Homo habilis

Rapid-FIRE?

DID NEANDERTHALS WEAR CLOTHES?

They probably wore rough cloaks made of fur.

Clothed in animal skins

DID EARLY HUMANS HUNT DINOSAURS?

No. Dinosaurs were extinct long before humans arrived.

WHAT IS THE EARLIEST CAVE PAINTING FOUND TO DATE?

A 44,000-year-old painting of wild pigs and buffaloes, found in a cave in South Sulawesi, Indonesia.

WHAT IS THE STUDY OF THE ORIGINS OF HUMANS CALLED?

Anthropogeny.

WHAT WAS THE STONE AGE?

Humans made tools out of stone until they discovered how to fashion them out of bronze about 5,500 years ago. The entire period, from the time of the earliest known stone tools, 3.3 million years ago, until the beginning of the Bronze Age, 5,500 years ago, is called the Stone Age.

HOW WAS AGRICULTURE A TURNING POINT IN HUMAN HISTORY?

When humans were inspired to raise their own crops, making them less dependent on foraging for wild plants, agriculture, the science of growing crops, was born. When humans first domesticated crops, 12,000 years ago, this focus also allowed them to settle down in one place instead of following a nomadic lifestyle. Agriculture thus became the basis of civilization, and the course of history was changed forever.

8000 BCE   3000 BCE

1830

Now

Agriculture then and now

Big ? WHAT WERE THE FIRST CROPS?

Archaeological evidence suggests that wild grains and berries were collected and eaten starting from around 20,000 BCE. The earliest farms were created in the Middle East around 10,000 years ago. Eight primary crops were the first to be domesticated: emmer wheat, einkorn wheat, hulled barley, peas, lentils, bitter vetch, chickpeas, and flax. They are called the Neolithic founder crops and were grown in the Middle East and Mediterranean regions. Wheat was the first crop to be grown and harvested on a large scale.

Emmer wheat

WHAT WERE THE FIRST INVENTIONS?

The Acheulean hand axe, a triangular, leaf-shaped rock, probably used for butchering animals, is the earliest known tool. Discovered in Kenya, it is about 1.7 million years old! Humans figured out how to start and control fire approximately 300,000 years ago. After settling in one place, they then started inventing more items to make life easier. Among the earliest were clay vessels for carrying water or cooking.

Acheulean hand axe

WHEN WERE ANIMALS FIRST DOMESTICATED?

When all animals ran wild, humans observed that some animals were easier to control and more useful than others. This marked the start of human-animal partnerships. Working with dogs began around 30,000 years ago, mostly for hunting. When farming became more popular, humans began to tame and breed animals, such as cattle and sheep, and use them for their milk.

Domesticated cattle in ancient Egypt

WHY WAS THE INVENTION OF THE WHEEL A LANDMARK IN HISTORY?

The wheel brought in many changes. The first wheels were for making pottery, but around 5,200 years ago, solid wheels were made for transportation. People discovered that wheels made travel faster and could even assist in carrying loads. This encouraged trade and industry. People started moving around as travelers and explorers.

Wooden block wheel

Rapid-FIRE ?

WHERE WAS RICE FIRST FARMED?

In the Yangtze River basin in China.

Rice cultivation

WHERE WAS CORN FIRST GROWN?

In Mexico, 9,000 years ago.

Cultivated corn

WHICH WERE THE FIRST CULTIVATED FRUITS?

Dates, olives, grapes, figs, and pomegranates, between 6000 and 3000 BCE.

Date palm

WHEN WAS THE STONE AGE?

The period between 3.3 million years ago to around 3000 BCE.

WHEN WAS THE BRONZE AGE?

From about 3300 BCE to 1200 BCE.

WHICH IS THE WORLD'S OLDEST CITY?

We don't know for certain, but Jericho, a Palestinian city in the West Bank region of Israel, is one of the oldest. The ruins of some of the old city walls date back over 11,000 years. They were probably massive structures made of stone and could have stood as tall as 23 feet. Archaeological evidence suggests that many other cities in the Middle East date back 7,000 years.

The ancient walls of Jericho

Big? WHAT WERE THE EARLY CITIES LIKE?

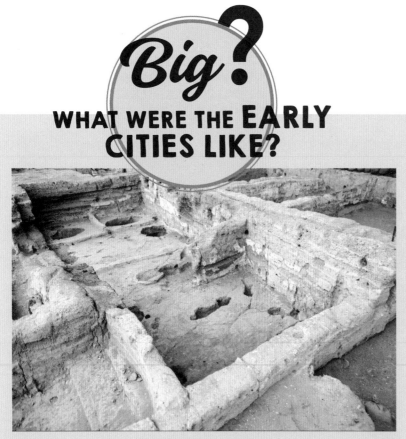

Çatalhöyük in Turkey

When humans began to settle, they probably did so in small groups. As the number of people increased, the small settlements grew and some became towns and cities. The first cities had a highly organized way of life, with rules and laws, as well as writing. The Indus Valley civilization in western South Asia had big, planned cities of more than 50,000 people. One of the world's oldest cities is Çatalhöyük in Turkey, with remains dating back to 6250 BCE. Its houses had an interesting feature—entry was through holes in the flat roofs!

DID THE INDUS VALLEY CIVILIZATION HAVE PLANNED CITIES?

The Indus Valley civilization (in modern Afghanistan, Pakistan, and India) had over 1,000 cities and settlements, mostly around the Indus River and its tributaries. They were well planned, with sanitation and trash collection, public granaries and baths. There were large walls and citadels. One port city, Lothal, even had a shipyard.

Stupa at Mohenjo-daro, Indus Valley civilization

WHO CREATED THE **FIRST ROOF GARDENS?**

Fresco of a king of Ur, Sumer

Six thousand years ago, the civilization of Sumer began to flourish on the fertile land between the Tigris and Euphrates Rivers in modern Iraq. The Sumerians built the great cities of Ur and Eridu. One of the centerpieces of Ur was the ziggurat, a pyramid-like structure used as a temple base. Trees, flowers, and lush gardens on each terrace of the enormous ziggurat provided a cool, shady place for visitors to rest.

WERE THERE ANY **CITIES IN ANCIENT CHINA?**

Chinese civilization began in the Yellow River valley around 10,000 BCE. The first towns emerged at Banpo, during 4800–3750 BCE. Banpo had round pit houses made with wood and mud, and thatched roofs. The town was surrounded by a moat for protection from hostile invaders.

Yellow River valley, China

*Rapid-*FIRE **?**

WHERE WERE THE ANCIENT CITIES OF **HARAPPA AND MOHENJO-DARO?**

They were part of the Indus Valley civilization.

Harappa, Indus Valley civilization

WHICH ANCIENT CITY WAS CARVED FROM DESERT STONE?

Petra, in Jordan.

Great Temple at Petra, Jordan

WHICH ANCIENT CIVILIZATION WAS BASED IN CRETE?

The Minoan, 3000–1100 BCE.

HOW OLD IS THE **NORTE CHICO CIVILIZATION OF PERU?**

It dates back to 3500 BCE, and lasted up to about 1800 BCE.

WHO SAILED AROUND THE WORLD FIRST?

In September 1519, a Portuguese explorer named Ferdinand Magellan led a Spanish expedition made up of five ships around the world for the first time. He sailed west, successfully crossing the Atlantic Ocean and the Pacific Ocean, but was killed near what is today known as the Philippines. Juan Sebastián Elcano brought what remained of the expedition party back to Spain in September, 1522—just one ship and 18 men.

Death of Ferdinand Magellan

WHO WERE THE FIRST EUROPEAN SETTLERS IN NORTH AMERICA?

Pedro Menéndez established the first European settlement, which was named St. Augustine, in Florida, in 1540. The area had been claimed for Spain by the Spanish explorer Juan Ponce de León when he landed there in 1513. The British, however, who arrived in North America in 1607, were much more successful in establishing their presence.

Fort at St. Augustine, Florida

Big? WHO DISCOVERED NEW ZEALAND?

Captain James Cook

The first settlers on New Zealand's islands were tribal Polynesian people from Hawaiki, ancestors of the Maori people. Maori legends say that Kupe, a fisherman and chief of Hawaiki, discovered the islands while he was exploring the Pacific Ocean. It was Dutch navigator Abel Tasman, the first of the European explorers to arrive in December, 1642, who named the land "Nieuw Zeeland." British naval captain James Cook landed in 1769, further opening up the islands to European settlement.

Vintage map of the world

HOW DID SAILORS CONTRIBUTE TO SCIENCE?

Those who sailed uncharted seas opened the doors to many discoveries. The explorers saw new things, made observations, and gathered information; they collected and brought back specimens of plants, animals, and soil. Very often, there were artists and scientists aboard who kept detailed records that helped in the growth of scientific knowledge. The preparation for these voyages also encouraged scientific thought and invention.

HOW LONG HAVE THE ABORIGINAL PEOPLE LIVED IN AUSTRALIA?

Aboriginal Australians, who have their own language and culture, are descendants of people who sailed from Asia 60,000 years ago and made this large island—which is also the smallest continent—their home.

Rapid-FIRE ?

WHY IS CHRISTOPHER COLUMBUS SO FAMOUS?

He was said to be the first European to sail to America.

Christopher Columbus

WHO NAMED THE PACIFIC OCEAN?

The Portuguese explorer Ferdinand Magellan called it *Mar Pacífico*, meaning "peaceful sea," because that's how it was when he sailed it.

HOW FAR WOULD YOU NEED TO SAIL TO GO AROUND THE WORLD?

At least 25,000 miles.

HOW DID ANCIENT SAILORS NAVIGATE?

By observing the Sun in the sky during the day and the North Star at night.

Ferdinand Magellan

WHO WERE THE FIRST SETTLERS IN NORTH AMERICA?

The earliest evidence of settlement is by the ancestors of today's Native Americans nearly 14,000 years ago. These people were nomadic tribes from Asia who entered the continent through Alaska. Before the Europeans landed in America, the Native Americans were already spread across in multiple communities with populations ranging from 10,000 to 200,000.

A group of Native Americans

The link between Asia and America

WHEN DID THE USA BECOME AN INDEPENDENT COUNTRY?

On July 4, 1776. That was when 13 English colonies made a declaration of independence from British rule to create a new nation: the United States of America. Later, Britain sent troops to take back the colonies but they were defeated in 1783.

The Liberty Bell

WHAT ARE TOTEM POLES?

The word "totem" means a mythical guardian spirit. Totem poles are carved and painted logs created by the Native Americans of the northwest US and Canada as an expression of respect. Mounted vertically in the ground, they depict different animals and spirits, and are a retelling of family legends through pictures.

Totem pole

WHAT WERE THE LIVES OF NATIVE AMERICANS LIKE?

Native Americans were hunter-gatherers as well as farmers. They kept dogs and used spears, harpoons, bows, and arrows, and other weapons made of stone. They grew a variety of plants and domesticated turkeys, llamas, and alpacas. Culturally, they were very diverse—the Arctic peoples were very different from those who lived on the plains.

A Native American horseman

Rapid-FIRE?

WHO LIVED IN TENTS ON THE GREAT PLAINS?

Native American tribes such as the Sioux and the Cheyenne.

A tribal tent

WHAT IS THE LIBERTY BELL?

Located in Philadelphia, this is the iconic bell that was rung in 1776 to declare America's independence.

WHY WAS THE BISON SO IMPORTANT FOR NATIVE AMERICANS OF THE PLAINS?

Their survival depended on it: from meat to skin, every part of the bison was put to use.

Bison

WHO WERE COWBOYS?

They were ranch workers who took care of cattle, and expert horse riders.

Cowboy

Big?

WHEN DID THE EUROPEANS FIRST ESTABLISH THEMSELVES IN NORTH AMERICA?

Statue of Sir Walter Raleigh in Greenwich, London

Spanish explorers were the first to settle in North America, after invading and colonizing present-day Florida and California starting in 1513. While the Spanish expanded their control in the south, the French sailed through North Carolina to present-day New York harbor in 1524, but, by 1565, the Spanish had destroyed the French colonies. Sir Walter Raleigh established the first British colony in North Carolina in 1585, though it did not do well. It was in 1607, when the British colony in Jamestown was set up (now in Virginia), that a new era began.

WHAT ARE ETHNIC GROUPS?

People belonging to the same geographical area, culture or nationality can be described as an ethnic group. They often share the same history and language. For example, people who come from the country of Japan, or have ancestors from Japan, are called Japanese people. The Han Chinese people are an East Asian ethnic group native to China.

Han people make up the world's largest ethnic group, approximately 18 percent of the global population. Today, many ethnic groups coexist together in one region.

Rapid-FIRE?

Maoris

WHO ARE THE **MAORI?**

The first people who settled in New Zealand around 1,000 years ago.

Inuit woman

WHO ARE THE **INUITS?**

Indigenous people inhabiting Arctic regions of Greenland, Alaska, and Canada.

Malay family

WHO ARE THE **MALAYS?**

People native to the Malay Peninsula, eastern Sumatra, and coastal Borneo, and the smaller islands between these locations.

WHERE ARE THE MOST CROWDED PLACES IN THE WORLD?

Large cities in small countries tend to be more crowded since millions of people move to urban centers to find jobs and a place to live. Bangladesh is one of the most crowded countries in the world, with more than 1,000 people per square mile.

Dhaka in Bangladesh

WHO ARE NOMADS?

Nomads are people with no fixed home. They travel from place to place with all their belongings, making fresh homes wherever they stop. Bedouins of the Sahara, Mongols of Asia, and the Masai of Africa are examples of nomadic people.

Mongols of central Asia

WHICH COUNTRY HAS THE LARGEST POPULATION?

More than 1.4 billion people currently live in China, which is more than anywhere else in the world. Most of the people here live in the big cities of the east and the south. Even in this most populated of countries there are areas, in the far west, where comparatively few people live, such as the Gobi Desert.

Crowded square in China

Big? HOW MANY PEOPLE LIVE IN THE WORLD?

A world full of people

Today, more than eight billion human beings live in the world. The first billion was reached around 1800, and the world's population has continued to increase rapidly ever since. During the 20th century, the human population grew from 1.65 billion to six billion! Since the start of the 21st century the birth rate has slowed down, and it is thought that the population will increase at a much slower rate now, and could peak at 11 billion in 2100.

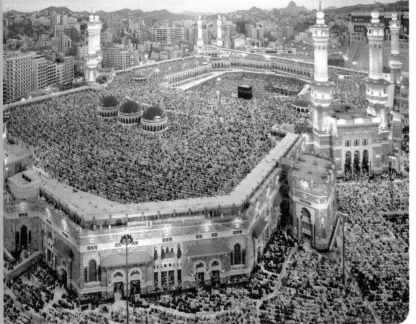

Pilgrims to the Great Mosque in Mecca at prayer

WHO ARE PILGRIMS?

Across the world, people of different religions travel to holy places, often on a long and difficult journey as a ritual to test and prove their belief. They are known as pilgrims.

Big?
WHICH CITY IS HOLY TO THREE FAITHS?

WHO WAS CONFUCIUS?

Confucius, also known as Kong Qiu, was a philosopher whose teachings have guided the people and government of China for centuries. He lived from 551 to 479 BCE and was a great scholar who emphasised the importance of education for all. Confucianism has influenced the way of life in China, Korea, Japan, and Vietnam.

The teachings of Confucius

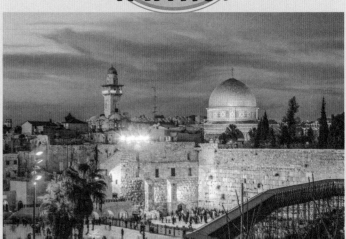

Old City of Jerusalem, Israel

Jerusalem, in Israel, is holy to Judaism, Islam, and Christianity. The sacred sites of Jerusalem include the Western Wall in the Jewish Quarter, revered by Jewish people because it is believed to be the remains of the ancient Temple of Solomon. For Christians, the Church of the Holy Sepulchre, location of the tomb of Jesus, is the holiest site. The Dome of the Rock, called Al-Haram ash-Sharif, is the most sacred site for Muslims, who believe the prophet Muhammad made his journey to heaven from there.

FOLLOWERS OF WHICH FAITH COVER THEIR MOUTHS?

Monks and nuns of the Jain religion in India, cover their mouths with masks. They practice strict nonviolence and don't want to harm even the tiniest of insects that could fly into their mouths if they are left uncovered.

Jain nuns

WHO HONORS THE FIVE "K'S"?

Followers of Sikhism, a religion founded by Guru Nanak, in Punjab, wear five items, all of which honor their faith, and begin with the letter "K." *Kesh* is uncut hair, *kanga* is a comb to carry, *kara* is a metal bangle to wear, *kirpan* is a small dagger, and *kaccha* is a kind of undergarment.

Sikh man

WHAT IS SHINTOISM?

It is the ancient religion of Japan. Also known as *kami-no-michi*, it is a religion tied to nature, with no founder, no sacred scriptures, but only beliefs passed down through generations.

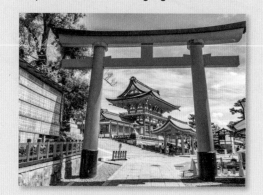

Gate to a Shinto shrine

Rapid-Fire ?

Breaking the fast after dusk during Ramadan

WHO FASTS DURING RAMADAN?

Muslims keep a strict fast from dawn to dusk during the holy month of Ramadan.

Ema tablets

WHAT ARE EMA TABLETS?

Wooden tablets with wishes written on them, left hanging at Shinto shrines.

Parsis

WHO ARE THE PARSIS?

The followers of the Zoroastrian religion that began in ancient Iran.

WHAT IS TAOISM?

A Chinese faith founded by Lao-tzu, around 2,500 years ago.

WHAT IS ISLAM?

Followers of the Islamic religion are called Muslims, and the Quran is the sacred scripture that guides them. Their place of worship is a mosque. The prophet Muhammad received the will of God and declared it to the people in Arabia in the seventh century. Muslims believe Allah is the one true God.

The Great Mosque at Mecca

Islamic calligraphy

Big?

HOW LARGE WAS THE ISLAMIC WORLD OF THE MIDDLE AGES?

In the Middle Ages, from about 700 to 1200 CE, the Islamic world included many different kingdoms and regions and this reflected a period of great power and high culture. The Muslim people were led by their religious leaders and were bound by commitment toward Islam. Islamic military leaders conquered and expanded their control on lands stretching from southern Spain to northwest India. Islamic traders traveled to far-off places such as southern Africa, China, and Russia, trading in silk, ivory, and spices.

WHAT IS AN ASTROLABE?

Astrolabe

A scientific instrument, originally from ancient Greece, the astrolabe was improved by Islamic astronomers of the Middle Ages into an amazing tool that enabled people to figure out the rising and setting of the sun, planets, and stars, and to calculate time.

WHICH ERA IS CALLED THE GOLDEN AGE OF ISLAM?

The Quran (Koran)

The period from 750 to 1258 CE, when the Abbasids were in power in Arabia, is known as the "golden age of Islam." Achievements in science, medicine, literature, and philosophy were at their height during this time in the Islamic world. In 1258, the Mongols captured Baghdad, bringing the golden age to an end.

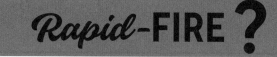

WHAT WERE THE CRUSADES?

The Crusades were a series of religious wars fought in the late 11th century between Christian and Muslim soldiers over the holy site of Jerusalem. Eight major Crusades took place between 1096 and 1291, ending with Middle Eastern powers taking control of the territory.

The Dome of the Rock, Jerusalem, Israel

WHAT IS ISLAMIC ART?

The term "Islamic art" refers to all the art, craft, and architecture created by Muslim craftspeople across the world. Calligraphy, the art of decorative writing, is an important part of Islamic art. It started with handwritten words from the holy Quran. Islamic art also has a lot of geometric patterns and floral motifs that decorate carpets, ceramics, books, and metal artifacts.

Friday Mosque, Herat, Afghanistan

Rapid-FIRE?

WHO LIVED IN THE ROUND CITY?

The citizens of Baghdad.

Al-Shaheed Monument, Baghdad

WHERE AND WHAT IS LA MEZQUITA?

The Great Mosque of Córdoba, Spain, built in 784 CE, and converted into a Christian cathedral in the 13th century.

La Mezquita

WHO WAS AVICENNA?

Called *Ibn Sina* in Arabic, he is regarded as one of the most significant scientists and philosophers of the golden age.

Avicenna

HOW LONG DID THE OTTOMAN EMPIRE LAST?

Nearly 700 years.

HOW DID CHINA GET ITS NAME?

Records of the Chinese civilization date as far back as the Shang dynasty of 1600 BCE. But it was in 221 BCE that Emperor Qin Shi Huang established the Qin dynasty, which unified the country for the first time in an empire that lasted until 206 BCE. The name "China" is derived from Qin, which is pronounced "Chin."

Emperor Qin
Shi Huang

WHO BUILT THE GOLDEN PAVILION?

Kinkaku-ji, the Golden Pavilion temple in Kyoto, Japan, was built in 1397 as the retirement villa of the shogun Ashikaga Yoshimitsu. After his death, it was converted into a Zen Buddhist temple. The temple, which is covered in gold leaf, sits in a beautiful natural landscape.

Kinkaku-ji, Japan

HOW OLD IS JAPANESE CIVILIZATION?

It is difficult to say how long people have lived in Japan. The earliest pieces of pottery found dates to the Jomon period of 10000 BCE. The Imperial Sun Dynasty of Japan was established in 660 BCE. The current emperor Naruhito is accepted as a descendant of the first Japanese emperor Jimmu, who was said to be descended from the sun goddess Amaterasu.

Jomon pottery

HOW DID CHINA PROSPER?

For centuries, China was one of the most advanced civilizations in the world. The Chinese made great progress in farming and engineering. They dug a vast network of irrigation channels, created foot-powered pumps to water the fields, and made their lands very productive. They knew the secrets of producing silk from silkworms, and they traded silk with the Western world, making themselves very wealthy. Under the Tang and Song dynasties (618–1279 CE), Chinese cities like Chang'an (modern Xi'an) were some of the world's largest.

WHAT IS THE
TERRA-COTTA ARMY?

When the tomb of Emperor Qin Shi Huang in the city of Xi'an, China, was excavated, a huge underground burial complex was discovered. It included an army of over 7,000 life-sized terra-cotta soldiers—each with a unique face and clothing—plus horses, chariots, armor, and weapons. It is believed that the emperor was obsessed with immortality and wanted to conquer death.

A few of the terra-cotta warriors

Rapid-FIRE ?

WHERE IS THE **FORBIDDEN CITY?**

The Forbidden City is in Beijing, China. It is a large palace complex that was built, and added to, by the Ming dynasty emperors from 1406 onward.

The Forbidden City, China

WHO WERE THE **SHOGUNS?**

They were military rulers in Japan from 1185 to 1868.

WHAT IS THE **NAME FOR CHINA IN THE CHINESE MANDARIN LANGUAGE?**

Zhongguo, which means "Middle Kingdom."

Big ?
WHO WERE THE
SAMURAI?

Samurai warrior

Samurai—the word means "those who serve"—were Japanese warriors who rose to power and rank in the 12th century. They followed a strict code of honor, discipline, and morality. For the samurai, honor mattered more than life and they would rather kill themselves than be defeated in a fight.

CAN CLOTHING IDENTIFY A PEOPLE?

These days, many people across the world wear T-shirts and jeans. There are, however, a number of countries and places where traditional clothes, identified with that specific area, are still worn. In many cultures, clothes indicate a person's social or religious position or whether or not they are married. Some clothes are reserved for special festivals or occasions like weddings. Others are used as casual or formal wear.

Japanese kimono

Evzones guarding the palace

DO EVZONES WEAR MODERN UNIFORMS?

Evzones are guards of honor at the Greek presidential palace. They are from the Greek army. Their uniform dates from the 19th century and includes a white skirt, wool leggings and a cap with a tassel.

Big? WHAT IS A KILT?

A kilt is a knee-length garment traditionally worn by the men of Scotland, and also by women and girls. Woven from wool, it has fixed pleats and is worn like a skirt. The colorful plaid fabric in a kilt is called tartan. A kilt pin holds the kilt in place. The kilt is accompanied by a small leather or fur bag around the waist called a sporran.

Kilt as part of traditional Scottish dress

HOW DID THE FRENCH BERET BECOME AN ICON OF FASHION?

In the 17th century, shepherds and peasants made flat, floppy hats of wool as a cheap head cover to beat the cold. Artists such as Rembrandt popularized these berets through their self-portraits. In the 20th century, the beret became highly fashionable, worn by actresses and many others. Interestingly, the beret has been favored by revolutionaries and war heroes too.

Beret

WHAT ARE CLOGS?

Clogs are wooden shoes that were worn by peasants in many parts of Europe. The Dutch are most associated with clogs, which were made from a single piece of alder wood. Both men and women wore them for protection from harsh weather. Farmers in the Netherlands still wear them.

Wooden clogs

WHAT DO PEOPLE WEAR AT SING-SINGS?

A *sing-sing* is a tribal festival of costume, music, and dance held in Papua New Guinea. It is a spectacular event that was started in 1957 and is attended by over 100 tribes from across the country.
The participants wear special costumes, jewelry and elaborate feathers, and paint their faces to symbolize the spirit of nature.

Sing-sing

Rapid-FIRE ?

WHAT IS A GHO?

It is a traditional dress worn by the men of Bhutan, consisting of a knee-length gown tied with a *kera* belt.

Man wearing a gho

WHAT IS A SHAPKA USHANKA?

A Russian fur cap with earflaps to beat extreme cold.

Shapka ushanka

WHERE DO WOMEN WEAR TALL LACE HATS?

Women in Brittany, northwest France, wear hats shaped like chimneys.

Breton lace hat

WHO INTRODUCED PERFECTLY FITTED TAILORED SUITS?

George Bryan "Beau" Brummell, in 19th-century London.

WHAT ARE CLOTHES MADE FROM?

Traditional Inuit coat made of seal and caribou fur

Clothes are made from all kinds of materials. They could be woven from natural fibers such as cotton or denim that come from plants. Some materials, such as wool, silk, leather, and fur, come from animals. Synthetic fabrics like polyester and nylon are from oil products, so are derived from fossil fuels.

HOW DOES A TUAREG DRESS?

The Tuareg are an ethnic nomadic group in the Sahara Desert of North Africa. The men, who are also called the "blue men of Sahara," wear a blue veil and cover their heads to protect themselves from the blistering heat—which is often more than 120 °F—and the dry sand.

Tuareg clothing

Big **?** WHAT IS THE STORY BEHIND JEANS?

Sewing a belt loop on jeans

Jacob Davis designed the shape, Levi Strauss supplied the fabric, and so jeans were invented—way back in 1873. Davis made the pants for one of his clients, who wanted a sturdy garment for rough wear. The jeans were made from a sturdy material called denim and the blue color came from a dye imported from India. To make them stronger, Davis placed copper rivets at the places where pants often rip: pockets and fastenings.

WHAT IS **BATIK?**

Making batik

Invented in Southeast Asia, batik is a way of making patterns on cloth. It involves putting wax on material in a pattern, then applying dye, which is only absorbed in the parts of the fabric without wax. Batik is a national art form in Indonesia, and patterns are handed down through generations of craftspeople.

WHERE DO **PANAMA HATS COME FROM?**

Panama hat

Panama hats were first made in Ecuador by interlacing the leaves of the toquilla palm. But the export of such hats around the world began in Panama, hence the name. If you look closely at the hat, you'll see that the palm fibers are very tightly woven in herringbone or diamond patterns.

WHAT CITY IS REGARDED AS **THE FASHION CAPITAL OF THE WORLD?**

Paris, in France—it has been a fashion center for hundreds of years. Milan, London, New York, and other major cities have also become famous for their high fashion and are known for staging shows of new fashions by innovative designers.

A fashion show in London

Rapid-FIRE **?**

WHAT IS A **SARAFAN?**

The traditional long dress worn by Russian girls, covering the body from neck to toe.

Traditional sarafan

WHAT IS A **SOMBRERO?**

The wide-brimmed hat of Mexico.

Boy in a sombrero

WHO **WEARS A CONICAL HAT?**

These are typically worn by farmers of China, Japan, Korea, Vietnam, and other Southeast Asian countries.

Traditional conical hat

WHICH PART OF THE WORLD DOES THE **DASHIKI BELONG TO?**

It is a colorful garment worn mostly in West Africa.

WHY ARE FESTIVALS CELEBRATED?

Festivals are occasions to express joy. Some mark important religious events, such as the festival of Christmas, which celebrates the birth of Jesus Christ. Other festivals are not religious in nature but celebrate events such as Navroz, the Parsi New Year and arrival of spring. There are also festivals purely for fun, like Spain's La Tomatina, where participants throw ripe tomatoes at each other!

La Tomatina, Bunol, Spain

Water festival, Myanmar

WHERE IS THE THINGYAN FESTIVAL HELD?

Thingyan is Myanmar's biggest festival, held around mid-April to celebrate the New Year. The Myanmarese believe that Thagyamin, the king of the nats (spirits), descends to Earth at this time and counts the good or bad deeds of people over the past year. On the eve of the festival, people throw water on each other.

Big ? WHAT IS THE FESTIVAL OF LIGHTS?

Celebrating Diwali

The Hindu festival of Diwali, celebrated mostly in India, is called the "festival of lights" because rows of oil lamps, candles, and twinkling electric lights are lit by people inside and outside their houses. The ancient festival celebrates the return of the Hindu god Rama to his kingdom. The goddess of good fortune, Laxmi, is also worshipped, and firecrackers are set off.

WHAT IS HANUKKAH?

In Hebrew, the word *hanukkah* means "to make something sacred," and the festival of the same name lasts for eight days. It is also a festival of light since families light a new candle each day on a special candlestick called a menorah. Hanukkah celebrates the recapture of the Jewish sacred temple in Jerusalem in ancient times. Scriptures are read, hymns are sung, and money is given to the poor at Hanukkah.

Lighting the menorah

WHERE DO DRAGONS DANCE?

Dragon dancing

The dragon is a symbol of power and luck in Chinese culture. On Chinese New Year, long dragon figures made of fabric or plastic are held up by people who crouch underneath, dancing and weaving the figures along the streets. Firecrackers are also set off to scare away evil spirits.

HOW DID HALLOWEEN BEGIN?

This fun festival's origins can be traced back to the Samhain festival of the ancient Celts. At this time, the spirits of the dead were believed to return to visit their homes, and the spirits of those who had died in the past year were meant to leave their homes and go to the next world.

Modern Halloween costumes

Rapid-FIRE ?

WHAT IS WESAK?

An important Buddhist festival to mark the Buddha's birth.

Marking Wesak

IS THERE A FESTIVAL FOCUSED ON CHEESE?

Yes, the Cooper's Hill Cheese-Rolling and Wake, near Gloucester, England.

Rolling cheese downhill

WHERE ARE ARTIFICIAL SPIDERS HUNG ON CHRISTMAS TREES?

In Ukraine.

Spider decoration

WHERE IS KING'S DAY CELEBRATED?

In the Netherlands— it celebrates King Willem-Alexander's birthday.

King's Day

Street dancer at the
MassKara festival,
Philippines

DO FESTIVALS CELEBRATE HISTORY?

Yes, many countries celebrate history, historical events, and personalities with festivals. Independence Day is marked across America by parades, fireworks, concerts, and family picnics. A city may celebrate its founding with a recreation of that era—Lugo in Spain brings history alive at the three-day Arde Lucus festival when its inhabitants dress up and transform the town into the original Roman settlement.

Big? WHAT IS A CARNIVAL?

St. Mark's Square Carnival, Venice, Italy

A carnival is an annual festival that is celebrated with parades, amusements such as street shopping and fairs, music, food, and dance. Carnival-like festivals have existed since ancient times. During the Roman festival of Saturnalia, dedicated to the god Saturn, all social norms were excused for a week, and people, including enslaved people, could behave just about any way they liked. The festive season before the Christian period of Lent is also known as Carnival.

WHO GETS TO SIT IN THE LEADER'S CHAIR?

In Turkey, on April 23, people celebrate the foundation of the Grand National Assembly in 1920. It is a public holiday that celebrates children of the world as future leaders. On this day, children take part in a cabinet meeting in the presidential palace. A "president" is selected from among the children, who even sits in the president's chair and addresses the country.

International Children's Day, Turkey

Feria de Abril, **Seville, Spain**

WHERE IS THE *FERIA DE ABRIL* HELD?

This cattle-trading fair is held in Seville, Spain. A temporary tent city is built near the Guadalquivir River, and people gather to watch flamenco dancing and bullfights. Andalusian horses are paraded, accompanied by ballads and guitar music.

WHAT IS A POWWOW?

A powwow is a get-together of the Native American people of the United States and the First Nations of Canada. It can be for a day or a week, with traditional dance and music. The beating of drums is given special importance.

Dancing at an annual powwow

WHY IS THE "FIFTH OF NOVEMBER" REMEMBERED?

On November 5, 1605, Guy Fawkes attempted to blow up the Houses of Parliament in England. His plot was discovered and stopped. There is a poem about it, with the lines "Remember, remember the fifth of November . . ." To commemorate the day, every year bonfires are lit, figures of Guy Fawkes are burned and fireworks are set off.

WHAT IS MARDI GRAS?

A carnival of spectacular parades—the one held in New Orleans is especially famous.

Mardi Gras parade

WHO WEARS GREEN ON ST. PATRICK'S DAY?

Irish people, who celebrate it as their national day.

St. Patrick's Day parade

WHAT ARE VENETIAN MASKS?

Ornately designed masks worn in Venice during carnivals.

Venetian masks

WHAT ARE THE ARTS OF A COUNTRY?

Every country is unique in its tradition and culture. The arts or art forms are the expressions of this uniqueness in the form of traditional and modern music, theater, dance, and the visual arts, such as paintings and movies. For example, flamenco dancers are traditionally identified with Spain, opera singers are associated with Italy, and Punch and Judy puppets belong to England.

Spanish flamenco dancers

WHERE DO THEY DANCE LIKE THE GODS?

In Kerala, a state in India, a dance-drama called Kathakali is performed in which dancers put on elaborate makeup that looks like masks, and wear gorgeous costumes and headgear to act out ancient tales of gods and demons. Some of the movements are taken from ancient Indian martial arts and sports.

Kathakali

Big?

WHAT IS KABUKI?

Kabuki performance

Kabuki is traditional Japanese theater, a style of dance, drama, and music accompanied by stunning stage design and props. The actors wear brilliant costumes and makeup. The word kabuki can be broken down into three characters: *ka* (sing), *bu* (dance) and *ki* (skill). Izumo no Okuni, a Shinto priestess, started performing kabuki around the city of Kyoto in the early 1600s. In those days, an all-female group portrayed both male and female characters.

WHO **CREATES PICTURES FROM SAND?**

The Navajo Nation of Arizona, Utah, and New Mexico in the US use colored sand to create 1,000 different designs. Sand paintings are not viewed as just art, but are respected as living beings with spiritual importance.

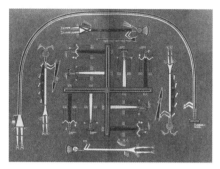

Navajo sand painting

IS THERE MORE THAN **ONE STRATFORD?**

Yes. Stratford-upon-Avon is in England, and is the birthplace of 16th-century playwright and poet William Shakespeare. In Ontario, Canada, there is a city called Stratford, which is famous for the Stratford Festival held every summer, where plays are performed in honor of Shakespeare. There are many more Stratfords around the world.

Stratford Festival Theatre, Ontario, Canada

WHAT IS A **MORRIS DANCE?**

This English folk dance dates back to the 15th century. Props such as sticks, swords, and handkerchiefs are clapped together by a group of dancers to the rhythm of the melodeon and drums. The dancers wear vests or tattered jackets, hats, and neckerchiefs.

Morris dancers

Rapid-Fire?

Khokhloma tableware

WHAT IS **KHOKHLOMA PAINTING?**

Russian wood painting with vivid patterns, created on tableware and furniture.

WHAT ARE **PANS?**

Pans are steel drums played by people of the Caribbean during carnivals.

Pan drums

IS IT **TRUE THAT SHIPS WERE NAMED** *MORRIS DANCE*?

Yes, two ships of the British Royal Navy in the 20th century.

WHO WERE THE VIKINGS?

From around 800 to 1100 CE, a large number of sea warriors from the extremely cold lands of Norway, Denmark, and Sweden started traveling to Britain, Europe, Iceland, Greenland, and Newfoundland, where they raided settlements. They came to be known as the Vikings.

Viking warrior ready for battle

A Viking raiding party

WERE THE VIKINGS FIERCE WARRIORS?

Yes, the Vikings were excellent sailors and fierce warriors. They sailed for thousands of miles across the icy northern oceans in open wooden boats known as longboats. They mostly looked for riches to loot, and they struck ruthlessly, killing, burning, and carrying away all that they could lay their hands on.

WHO WAS LEIF ERIKSON?

Leif Erikson was a bold adventurer from a Viking colony who sailed westward from Greenland until he reached a place which he named Vinland, because of the grapes growing there. Vinland was probably the region of present-day New Brunswick, Canada. The son of Eric the Red, Leif is believed to have been the first European to sail to and explore North America.

WHAT DID THE VIKINGS SEIZE ON THEIR RAIDS?

The Vikings specialized in hit-and-run raids. They seized all kinds of treasure. In 1840, in Lancashire, England, a hoard of silver, including coins and belt buckles, believed to have been buried by the Vikings in the 10th century, was discovered. The Vikings even kidnapped people to sell as slaves.

Part of the Viking hoard found buried in England

Viking raiders

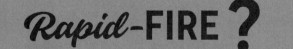

Big?
WHAT DOES "VIKING" MEAN?

Vik is an Old Norse word that also means bay or creek, and from it comes the word "viking," meaning pirate. The Vikings were considered sea pirates who came and looted monasteries and wealthy European kingdoms, so the name is mostly linked with their actions. Not all Vikings were pirates, however; some were traders and settlers too. The Vikings did not belong to any particular tribe and were mostly farmers when not at sea.

Rapid-FIRE?

WHAT MARKED THE END OF THE VIKING AGE?

In England, the defeat of the last Viking king, Harald Hardrada of Norway, but some Vikings remained until the 15th Century.

Bust of King Harald

WHO WAS ERIC THE RED?

He was the founder of a new settlement to the west of Iceland, a place that he named Greenland.

DID THE VIKINGS BELIEVE IN GOD?

They had many gods, such as Thor, Odin, and Freya.

The Viking god Odin

WHAT WERE VIKING SHIPS MADE OF?

Long and narrow flexible strips of wood attached to a wooden backbone called a keel.

Viking longboats

HOW ANCIENT IS ANCIENT EGYPT?

Fresco showing agricultural activities

Ancient Egypt was a majestic civilization that grew up around the Nile River in northeastern Africa in about 3100 BCE. The fertile soil along the Nile made Egypt a rich crop-growing area. This allowed trading, which led to even more prosperity, and the development of a complex, fascinating civilization that now has a complete field of study dedicated to it called Egyptology.

HOW WERE THE PYRAMIDS BUILT?

Pyramids were built to last. Massive stone blocks were moved across the desert from the quarry by thousands of laborers. Craftsmen chiseled the stone into smaller blocks, which were then lifted and fit into place. It is believed that the Egyptians knew the technique of wetting sand to the exact amount that made it easier to pull stone blocks over it.

Pyramids at Giza

Big ? WHAT WAS SO SPECIAL ABOUT ANCIENT EGYPT'S CULTURE?

The Sphinx at Giza

The highly developed civilization excelled in architecture and other crafts. Many of its archaeological sites, including the Great Pyramid and other huge monuments, are still standing. These buildings are proof of technical expertise and the employment of a huge and well-organized workforce. Many buildings carry rows of a complex writing that is made up of pictures, known as hieroglyphs. The ancient Egyptians had many gods, and the pharaoh, or king, was also regarded as a god on earth. The beautiful Egyptian art depicts their gods and the lives of pharaohs.

WHY WERE THE PYRAMIDS BUILT?

Since the pharaohs were considered to be human gods who returned to the heavens after death, elaborate tombs, called pyramids, were built as their burial chambers. These were filled with many objects that were important to the pharaoh.

Treasures found in Tutankhamun's tomb in the Valley of the Kings

WHAT ARE MUMMIES?

Mummies are preserved bodies. Dead pharaohs and nobles were mummified (preserved in a highly specialized way) before being put in the tomb. First the body was washed, and then, after the internal organs were removed, it was packed with salt and left until it dried out completely. The dry skin was then rubbed with oils and potions and carefully wrapped in a resin-soaked linen bandage. The mummy was finally placed inside a beautifully decorated coffin called a "sarcophagus."

A mummy wrapped in linen

Rapid-FIRE?

WHO WAS NEFERTITI?

She was a renowned beauty and the queen of Pharaoh Akhenaten.

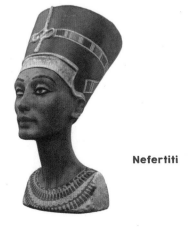

Nefertiti

WHAT IS AMAZING ABOUT THE INNER SARCOPHAGUS OF TUTANKHAMUN?

The fact that it is made of 240 lbs of gold!

Burial mask of Tutankhamun

HOW OLD IS THE GREAT PYRAMID OF GIZA?

4,500 years!

HOW LONG DID THE PROCESS OF MUMMIFICATION TAKE?

About 70 days.

WHAT WAS SPECIAL ABOUT ANCIENT GREECE?

The ancient Greek civilization's amazing achievements in art, architecture, politics, science, and philosophy had a tremendous influence on Western civilization as a whole, and continue to play a big role even today. The revolution in thinking and creativity that occurred from around 700 BCE to 480 BCE in Greece had a monumental impact on all walks of life.

Ruins of the Sanctuary of Athenea Pronea, Delphi, Greece

WHY DID THE GREEKS BUILD TEMPLES?

The Greeks worshipped many gods and goddesses because they believed they had special powers, so temples were built to honor them. Visitors would pray and hope the gods and goddesses would grant them their wishes.

Big ? WHY IS ANCIENT ROME CONSIDERED SUCH A GREAT CIVILIZATION?

The Roman civilization was one of the most powerful in the history of humanity, with outstanding military and political skills. From its beginnings as a small town on the Tiber River in central Italy in the eighth century BCE, Rome became the heart of an enormous empire that spread across Europe, Britain, western Asia, northern Africa, and the Mediterranean islands. Spoken Latin shaped many modern European languages, such as Italian, French, Spanish, Portuguese, and Romanian. We also owe the 26-letter alphabet and the 12-month calendar used today to ancient Rome.

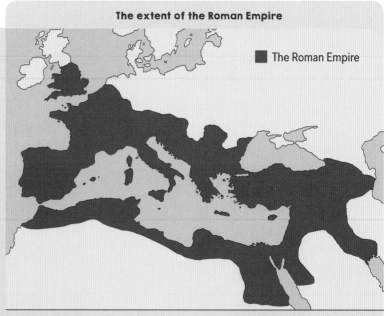

The extent of the Roman Empire

■ The Roman Empire

WHO FOUNDED ROME?

According to myth, the twin brothers Romulus and Remus, sons the Roman god of war, Mars, were suckled and kept alive by a she-wolf who found the babies abandoned in a forest. When the boys grew up, they established a city at the site in 753 BCE. The city was called "Rome" after Romulus, the first ruler.

Romulus, Remus, and the she-wolf

WHO STARTED THE OLYMPIC GAMES?

Greek stamp depicting the ancient Olympics

In 776 BCE, the Greeks started an athletic competition in the city of Olympia, which was held every four years. Athletes from all over Greece competed in various events, including running, boxing, and wrestling. This sporting event was the origin of today's Olympic Games.

WHAT MADE JULIUS CAESAR A GREAT RULER?

Ancient Rome was a republic with officials who were voted for by the people. All this changed in 45 BCE when Julius Caesar declared himself supreme ruler. He became the first Roman dictator, and with his extreme military might and enormous wealth began a new era of the Roman Empire.

Rapid-FIRE ?

WHAT IS HADRIAN'S WALL?

Built by the Roman emperor Hadrian across the north of Britain, the wall guarded the frontiers of the Roman Empire.

Hadrian's Wall

WERE THE ANCIENT GREEKS FOND OF THEATRE?

Yes, they built theaters in almost every city, and some could accommodate thousands of people.

Amphitheater in Delphi, Greece

Bronze statue of Julius Caesar, Rome, Italy

WHO WERE THE INCAS?

In the 15th and 16th centuries BCE, the Incas ruled an enormous kingdom in the Andes mountains of South America. Their military might was supreme. The Inca Empire covered today's Peru, Ecuador, Bolivia, Chile, and northwest Argentina. It spread over 2,000 miles, included 12 million people and 100 different ethnic groups, and connected them all with an excellent road system.

Ancient Maya citadel at Tikal, Guatemala

WHO WERE THE MAYA?

The Maya civilization was the most dominant around Mexico and Central America, dating back to 1800 BCE. In 250 CE, during what was the golden age of the Maya civilization, there were as many as 40 highly developed Maya cities.

Hand-carved Maya mask

Big? WHO WERE THE AZTECS?

Huitzilopochtli, god of the sun and water

The Aztecs, also called Tenochca, ruled the most densely populated empire in the 15th century BCE, covering an area that stretched across today's central and southern Mexico. They were a hunting tribe that settled on islands in Lake Texcoco and made Tenochtitlan their capital city. Gradually, based on a highly developed agricultural system, they built up a very prosperous empire that lasted over 100 years. The Aztecs worshipped Huitzilopochtli, the god of sun and water. Every Aztec male was a warrior, and prisoners of war were killed as sacrifices to the gods.

WHAT IS UNIQUE ABOUT AZTEC ART?

Aztec art and craft was beautifully detailed. Aztecs made huge stone and wood sculptures of gods. Smaller pieces were carved in jade and quartz, and turquoise and mother-of-pearl were used to cover the sculptures. The Aztecs were also skilled potters, though the potter's wheel was not known to them. They used bright colorful bird feathers to adorn their headdresses and military shields.

Aztec sculpture

DID THE MAYA BUILD PYRAMIDS?

The temples built by the Maya in the center of their cities were shaped like pyramids. El Castillo in Chichén Itzá in the Yucatán is built of stone and has 365 steps leading to the temple at the peak. There was also an astronomical observatory at the top.

El Castillo, Chichén Itzá

Galleons like this brought the Spanish to South America

*Rapid-*FIRE ?

WHICH IS THE MOST IMPORTANT INCA SITE?

Machu Picchu, located in the Andes mountains in Peru.

Machu Picchu

WHY WAS THE LLAMA SO IMPORTANT FOR THE INCAS?

The llama, a camel-like animal, is adapted to the harsh cold and wind, so it became the Incas's beast of burden, and also provided wool.

A llama

WHAT IS NAHUATL?

The Aztec language, which gave words to Spanish and English such as "chili," "chocolate," "guacamole," and "avocado."

WHY DID THE POWER OF THESE CIVILIZATIONS DECLINE?

When the Spanish explorers reached South America, they brought with them diseases such as smallpox, against which the native population had no immunity. As a result, many died.
The Spanish, who attacked first in search of gold and riches and then established colonies, eventually conquered the region.

WHEN WERE THE MIDDLE AGES?

The period in Europe after the fall of the Roman Empire in 476 CE and before the Renaissance in the 14th century is called the Middle Ages. At this time, kings, queens, and nobles ruled the different countries, but the ordinary people lived in poverty.

Painting showing the king, doctors (in masks), and monks all helpless against the Black Death

WHAT WAS THE **BLACK DEATH?**

The disease known as bubonic plague killed about 25 million people in Europe between 1347 and 1351. It was easily spread between people, which meant that the overcrowded cities saw a much greater number of deaths. The disease was much feared because seemingly healthy people would go to bed one night and be found dead in the morning.

Big?
WHO WAS THE VIRGIN QUEEN?

From 1558 to 1603, Queen Elizabeth I ruled England. This was a time when most people believed women were weak and could not rule a kingdom. Elizabeth never married and so she was called the Virgin Queen. She was a great leader and, during her rule, politics, commerce, and the arts flourished—her reign is widely accepted as the height of English Renaissance. Despite the almost continuous threat to her position from among her own nobles, she brought the country together against foreign powers. Her power was such that the 16th century in England is known as the Elizabethan Age.

Queen Elizabeth I

WHAT WAS **RURAL LIFE LIKE DURING THE MIDDLE AGES?**

Europe in the Middle Ages was a feudal society. This meant that the king granted land holdings, known as fiefs, to nobles. Landless peasants, called serfs, worked on these fiefs, living in poverty, since the larger share of the crops produced was taken by the nobles and the king as tax.

HOW DID KNIGHTS PROTECT THEMSELVES?

During the Middle Ages, it was customary for men from noble families to be trained as knights—to fight and lead soldiers into battles. In 1000, knights wore simple chain-mail tunics. By about 1450, they wore full body armor, made of shaped metal plates. The armor of higher-ranking nobility was often decorated with engraved patterns or polished gold.

A knight in armor

WHAT KIND OF BUILDINGS WERE BUILT DURING THE MIDDLE AGES?

The Middle Ages saw the building of great cathedrals and the introduction of a new, Gothic, architectural style, in which buildings had huge, tall windows, pointed ceilings, and arches. Wall paintings and mosaics decorated the interiors along with paintings.

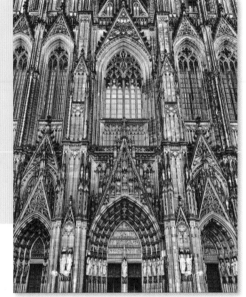

Gothic facade of the cathedral in Cologne, Germany

Rapid-FIRE ?

WHAT IS NOTRE DAME?

A Gothic-style, Catholic cathedral in Paris, France, built in 1160.

The cathedral at Notre Dame

WHO LIVED IN CASTLES?

Lords and noblemen lived in large, strong castles built of stone, at the top of hills. This protected them from enemy attack.

Gravensteen castle, Belgium

WAS KNIGHTHOOD A TITLE TO BE EARNED?

Yes, either through bravery in battle or by successful training under a knight.

HOW DID TRADE AND CULTURE EVOLVE IN AFRICA?

Africa's trade and culture developed between 750 and 1500 CE. It was one of the richest continents and its merchants traveled as far as India and Southeast Asia. Gold, ivory, ebony, and enslaved people from the West African kingdoms of Ghana, Mali, and Songhai were traded for salt and copper.

A gold nugget from Africa

WHO WERE THE MUGHALS?

The Mughal Empire dominated much of the Indian subcontinent during the later medieval period. It was founded by Babur, a Turkish-Mongol chieftain. His descendants, such as Akbar and Shah Jahan, built the empire with many military victories. The Mughal period was one of great wealth and cultural splendor.

Emperor Shah Jahan

Big?

WHICH AFRICAN CITY HAD A FAMOUS UNIVERSITY?

Sankore Mosque, Timbuktu, Mali

Sankore University in Timbuktu, central Mali, was renowned, particularly for its library of nearly 70,000 manuscripts. Sundiata Keita, who was also called the "Lion King," brought Mali great prosperity, wealth, gold, and luxurious lifestyles through trade. Timbuktu, on the banks of the Niger River, became a big center for Muslim learners, scholars, and teachers. It had several mosques to practice and learn the faith, and markets dedicated to handwritten books.

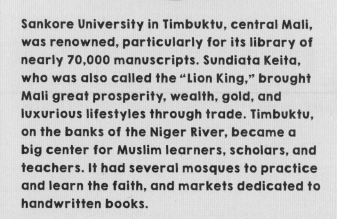

Rapid-FIRE ?

WHERE IS THE GOLDEN TEMPLE?

In Amritsar, Punjab, India. It is the main shrine of the Sikh religious faith.

Golden Temple, Amritsar

WHAT WERE DHOWS?

Trading ships from East Africa.

Dhow at sea

WHAT WAS THE CHOLA DYNASTY OF SOUTH INDIA FAMOUS FOR?

Its naval power and bronze sculptures.

WHO RULED INDIA DURING THE MEDIEVAL PERIOD?

The medieval period in India stretched from about 750 to 1750 CE. During the early part, India had a number of dynasties in power—the Rajputs, Delhi Sultanate, Palas, Chalukyas, and Pallavas, to name a few. Each controlled their own region and fought battles to gain control of land and wealth.

Part of the ruins of the Chalukyan capital at Badami, India

WHAT WAS THE GREAT ZIMBABWE?

It was the capital city of an African empire that extended over present-day Botswana, Zimbabwe, and Mozambique, between the 13th and the 15th centuries. The city's enormous fortress had stone towers and walls, the remains of which can still be seen. At its peak, it is estimated to have been home to 20,000 people.

Fortress of Great Zimbabwe

WHAT IS THE TAJ MAHAL?

It is the most famous example of Mughal architecture in India. Built by Emperor Shah Jahan in the 17th century as a tomb for his beloved wife Mumtaz, it is a pure-white marble structure decorated with gold and semiprecious stones. Twenty thousand skilled workers took 22 years to build it.

Taj Mahal, Agra

WHO WERE THE MONGOLS?

Central Asia—the Mongolian plateau in particular—was home to a number of nomadic tribes with a common language and culture, who were known as the Mongols. They were renowned warriors, skilled horsemen and archers. United under Genghis Khan in 1206, they defeated armies in Iran, Russia, Eastern Europe, and China to build the Mongol Empire.

Genghis Khan

WHO WERE THE SCYTHIANS?

They were nomads who migrated west from Central Asia around the eighth and seventh centuries BCE. The Scythians built a rich and powerful empire around what is now Crimea that lasted for many centuries.

Scythian mounted archer

WHY WAS GENGHIS KHAN SUCH A REMARKABLE PERSON?

Genghis Khan, emperor of the Mongols, is legendary not only among Mongols but also across the rest of the world. He selected his best men on the basis of merit and not lineage, and was tolerant toward all religions. He often gave his enemies the option of surrendering and signing a peace treaty—but if they resisted he was ruthless, sometimes destroying the entire tribe. He set up a highly efficient postal-rider system called the "Yam." He was a military genius and a brilliant leader of men, who established one of the largest empires in history.

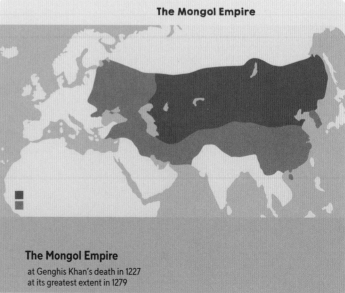

The Mongol Empire

The Mongol Empire
at Genghis Khan's death in 1227
at its greatest extent in 1279

WHO WAS **ALEXANDER NEVSKY?**

He was the grand prince who protected Russia—a great Russian diplomat and soldier who collaborated with the Mongols to defeat Swedish and German knights. This prevented a takeover of Russia by the Western world during the Battle of Neva, in 1240, and the Battle on the Ice, in 1242.

Monument to Alexander Nevsky and his soldiers

WAS **MOSCOW ALWAYS A POWERFUL CITY?**

Around 1200, when Russia was under Mongol rule, Moscow was a small trading town and center for tax collection. In 1326, the head of the Russian Orthodox Church moved to Moscow soon it became the center of power. Gradually, the local princes extended their influence in the neighboring areas.

The Kremlin, Moscow

WHO WAS TITLED "THE TERRIBLE"?

Ivan IV, who became tsar of Russia in 1547. He was a ruthless ruler who killed anyone who opposed him. He even killed his own son in a fit of rage. The nobles and the army all worked toward controlling rebellions in Ivan's kingdom and were rewarded for loyalty of service.

Statue of Ivan the Terrible

Rapid-FIRE **?**

WHICH **CULTURE AND FAITH INFLUENCED RUSSIA THE MOST?**

The Byzantine culture and the Eastern Orthodox Christianity it followed.

St. Basil's Cathedral in Moscow

WHAT WAS THE **ORIGINAL NAME OF RUSSIA?**

Kievan Rus, where Kiev was the capital city, and Rus was derived from the name of a Viking or Slav tribe that established the first Russian state in the ninth century.

WHO WERE THE **COSSACKS?**

They were people who lived north of the Baltic and Caspian Seas and were famous as fine soldiers.

WHERE IS OCEANIA?

Oceania is the collective name given to all the islands that are spread across the Central and South Pacific Ocean. The population excedes 12 million people, with more than 10,000 Oceanian islands, including Australia, New Zealand, and Melanesia.

Taiwan

Philippines

Asia

Palau

Micronesia

Marshall Islands

Federated States of Micronesia

Nauru

Indonesia

Papua New Guinea

Solomon Islands

Melanesia

Vanuatu

Tuvalu

Kiribati

Samoa

Fiji

Tonga

Cook Islands (N Z)

Hawaii (USA)

French Polynesia (France)

Polynesia

Australia

Australasia

New Zealand

Oceania

HOW WERE THE POLYNESIAN ISLANDS COLONIZED?

The first Christian missionaries arrived in early 1800, and with them began the era of colonization. Britain, France, Germany, New Zealand, United States, and Chile all colonized islands in the region and it was a period of great struggle for the native peoples to retain their indigenous culture and way of life.

Big? IS POLYNESIA ONE ISLAND?

Polynesia is a triangular area in the east-central Pacific Ocean marked by the Hawaiian islands in the north, New Zealand (Aotearoa) in the west, and Easter Island (Rapa Nui) in the east. Within this area there are also many smaller islands. People first settled here around 3,000 years ago. Hostile conditions on the islands made the settlers excellent sailors, fishermen, and farmers as they had to work hard to make the most of the existing resources, but, as their beautiful wood carvings show, they were also amazing craftspeople.

Ancient Polynesian-style carvings on a beach

Crafting a canoe

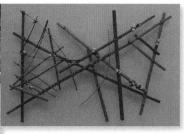

Micronesian navigational chart

HOW DID THE POLYNESIANS CROSS THE PACIFIC OCEAN?

Settled on islands in the middle of an ocean, the Polynesians developed outstanding boat building and navigational skills. Having studied the waves and stars, and with maps made out of twigs and shells, they sailed and paddled big outrigger canoes across the Pacific Ocean.

WHAT WAS THE TREATY OF WAITANGI?

Signed on February 6, 1840, between the Maori chiefs of New Zealand and the British, this agreement gave the queen of England the right to rule over New Zealand, but allowed land ownership to be retained by the Maoris. By the 20th century, however, and after many conflicts, the British took majority control over the islands.

Treaty of Waitangi

Maori of New Zealand

WHO WAS KAMEHAMEHA I?

Also called Kamehameha the Great, Kamehameha I was a strong, shrewd king who unified the Hawaiian islands in the late 18th and early 19th centuries. He outlawed human sacrifice, traditionally performed to increase the power of the king. He also promoted trade in sandalwood, which brought prosperity to the islands.

Kamehameha I

Rapid-FIRE ?

WHO IS KU-KA'ILI-MOKU?

The Hawaiian god of war.

The god Ku-ka'ili-moku

HOW LONG WERE POLYNESIAN CANOES?

About 100-150 ft.

Samoan canoe

WHERE DID PEOPLE FIRST SETTLE IN POLYNESIA?

On the islands of Wallis, Futuna, Samoa, and Tonga.

HOW MANY LANGUAGES ARE SPOKEN IN POLYNESIA?

Approximately 30, including Samoan, Maori, Tahitian, Hawaiian, and Tongan.

WHAT WAS THE INDUSTRIAL REVOLUTION?

In the 18th century in Britain, the introduction of large-scale production using machines transformed human society. People left agricultural lifestyles and migrated to cities to work in factories. Not only did this industrialization change how things were produced, but also what was produced and what it cost. All this had a huge impact on how people lived—in fact, it changed the face of the world. That is why it is called the Industrial Revolution.

Mechanized, assembly-line production

WHO WORKED IN THE FIRST FACTORIES?

Starting in the mid 1700s, factories began to be built in Britain. The machines were owned by powerful businessmen known as industrialists, and staffed by workers who were paid for the number of hours they worked. Textile factories were the first to be set up, and a large number of women and children found employment in them.

The spinning room of a textile mill, Massachusetts, USA

Rapid-FIRE ?

WHO INVENTED THE STEAM ENGINE?

Several people contributed, but James Watt was a key figure.

James Watt

WHAT WAS STEPHENSON'S ROCKET?

A powerful steam locomotive built by George Stephenson in 1829.

Stephenson's Rocket

WHEN WAS THE FLUSH TOILET INTRODUCED?

The 19th century, in London.

DID CHILDREN WORK IN FACTORIES?

Yes, children worked as many as 16 hours a day in factories and in mines. They breathed chemical fumes and coal dust, and a large number died either due to accidents or the very poor conditions they worked in. In 1802, the British government passed laws to protect child workers.

Young boys in a workshop

DID BRITAIN TRY TO KEEP MACHINES SECRET?

Yes, realizing the enormous potential of their machines and methods, Britain tried to keep the manufacture and use of machines a closely guarded secret. But industrial spying was common and the smuggling of machines was also attempted. Very soon, other European countries were setting up their own factories and railroads.

Heavy industrial machinery

WHY WERE DRAINS AND TOILETS SO IMPORTANT?

As workers started crowding industrial towns, houses were built quickly and cheaply to accommodate them. Toilet and drainage facilities were not properly considered. Waste was collected and dumped into nearby rivers. Epidemics and sickness became frequent until proper hygiene was introduced.

Big?

HOW DID RAILROADS CHANGE THE WORLD?

Steam locomotive

Horse-drawn wagons on wooden rails had been used to carry coal and stones from mines and quarries since the 16th century, but it was the invention of the steam engine that brought about the biggest change. Steam engines pulling cars on metal rails could transport raw materials and goods faster, helping trade and industry to expand. Quicker, easier, and cheaper transportation meant finished products could now reach newer places; for instance, fresh farm produce could be sent to cities, which had not been possible before. Passenger trains made it easier for greater numbers of people to travel farther and faster.

WHAT IS THE MODERN AGE?

The 20th century saw many remarkable changes. The period that began at the end of World War I saw many technical revolutions but, with newer, more powerful weapons came even more destructive wars, including the ravages caused by atomic bombs. Humans explored space and walked on the Moon, but millions on Earth still suffer hunger and poverty.

Astronaut walking on the moon

Big? WHICH GREAT MODERN AGE INVENTIONS CHANGED THE WORLD?

Colossus

Many amazing discoveries and inventions have been made. Pressurized cabins were developed in 1944, which made high-altitude, long-distance air travel possible. The life-saving antibiotic drug penicillin was discovered in 1928, changing the treatment of infections. V2 became the first of the modern rockets and enabled later space exploration sciences. Radar improved monitoring and prevented attacks. The first atom bomb, although highly destructive, led to humans harnessing nuclear power. Then there was the first computer—Colossus—and those that followed changed everything about the world as we knew it.

WHAT WAS THE COLD WAR?

The 1940s to the 1980s was a time of tension between a capitalist USA and a communist USSR (now Russia), who had contrasting political views and opposed each other on almost every front. While the two powers never fought a direct battle, their distrust created a lot of conflict around the globe.

Cold War tensions

WHAT WAS THE **LONG MARCH?**

Starting in October, 1934, approximately 100,000 Chinese communists under the leadership of Mao Tse-tung endured hardship and starvation to march nearly 5,000 miles across the country, reaching out to the people wherever they went. Mao, who became the undisputed leader and ruler of China in 1949, halted the Long March in October, 1935.

Mao Tse-tung

WHO DROPPED THE
FIRST ATOMIC BOMB?

The USA, with the consent of the Allies, dropped the first atomic bomb on the Japanese city of Hiroshima on August 6, 1945, bringing an end to World War II. The bomb instantly killed 70,000 people and over 100,000 had died by the end of the year from the effects of the bomb. The impact of nuclear radiation continued to affect many for years after the bombing.

Hiroshima after the bombing

WHO MADE FIVE-YEAR PLANS?

Joseph Stalin, who led the Soviet Communist Party from 1924 to 1953, made Five-Year Plans to reorganize, industrialize and develop the USSR. Under his leadership, thousands of factories were developed and large-scale shared farms were organized.

Joseph Stalin

Rapid-FIRE **?**

WHO WAS BUZZ ALDRIN?

The second man to step on the Moon, right behind Neil Armstrong.

Buzz Aldrin

DID THE **FIRST ATOMIC BOMB HAVE A NAME?**

It was called "Little Boy" and was dropped from a B-29 bomber airplane named Enola Gay.

Model of "Little Boy"

WHICH **TWO** COUNTRIES LED THE SPACE RACE?

The USSR and the USA.

Flags of the USA and the USSR

WHAT IS A GOVERNMENT?

A government is a group of people who set the laws and rules by which a country is run. These laws and rules control everything from businesses to schools and hospitals, and they set out limits for our behavior. There are many forms of government across the world, reflecting the many different types of countries with varied cultures and histories.

The British Houses of Parliament, Westminster Palace, London, UK

WHO IS A HEAD OF STATE?

The most important person in a country is the head of state. This may be the king or a queen or an elected president. The head of state represents the country and takes part in ceremonies with other countries.

Motorcade of a head of state

Big? WHAT ARE THE VARIOUS TYPES OF GOVERNMENT?

Democracy

Dictatorship

Aristocracy

Monarchy

Types of government

There are four major types of government. In an aristocracy, wealth or land ownership decides who is most powerful and able to set the rules for others. In a monarchy, the king or the queen holds absolute power. In a democracy, the people rule themselves by choosing their own representatives to form a government. Some countries are ruled by dictators, where one person assumes the power to make any decision, with or without the approval of the government or the people. Anarchy is a society without government.

WHO IS **QUEEN ELIZABETH II?**

The former queen of the United Kingdom.

Elizabeth II

WHAT IS A **PARLIAMENT?**

A meeting place for the government to discuss, approve and reject proposed policies.

A parliament in session

WHICH IS THE **WORLD'S OLDEST ROYAL FAMILY?**

The Japanese royal family has had a long line of 125 reigning emperors over a period of more than 2,500 years!

Emperor Naruhito and Empress Masako of Japan

HOW DOES A PERSON BECOME **KING OR QUEEN?**

Usually, by birth.

WHAT ARE **CAPITALISM, SOCIALISM, AND COMMUNISM?**

Capitalism is an economic system dedicated to growth and making more money. Everyone is free to own their own business and resources, employ people, and sell the product of the business for the best price possible. Businesses compete to make more profit. In socialism, the people who work are the ones who own the businesses. Often, the government collects profit and distributes it among everyone. In a communist system, the government owns the businesses and is supposed to assure a minimum standard of living to everyone, whatever they earn.

American War of Independence

WHAT IS A **REPUBLIC?**

A country that has no king or queen as the head of state. France is a republic. During a revolution over 200 years ago, the French king was executed, and ever since there has been no royal rule in France. The USA was ruled by the British king until the American Revolutionary War, 1776-1783.

WHY DO LAWS DIFFER BETWEEN COUNTRIES?

Voters at a polling station, Great Britain

Laws are a system of rules that govern the citizens of a country. Laws are shaped by a nation's political, religious, financial, and social structures, along with culture and traditions. The rules of law are created by governments and lawmakers and can change with time and according to who is in government.

WHERE DO **JUDGES WEAR WIGS?**

Judges wear big, old-fashioned wigs in Great Britain. Wigs started appearing as the dress code of high society in the 17th century. After the 18th century, when they were no longer fashionable, courts continued with the practice, especially as a ceremonial dress reserved for the highest authority of law.

Judge in his wig

Big **?**

WHO **INTRODUCED DEMOCRACY?**

The word "democracy" comes from ancient Greek, where *demos* means "common people" and *kratos* means "strength." In the sixth century BCE, a statesman named Cleisthenes introduced this reformed political system in Athens. According to this system, all Athenian citizens were part of the assembly and had a vote in the making of laws. Women, citizens below 20 years old, enslaved people, and foreigners were, however, excluded.

Cleisthenes

WHAT IS INTERNATIONAL LAW?

While every country makes laws for its citizens, and for foreigners participating in its affairs, there are some legal rules, standards, and norms that are agreed to jointly by almost all sovereign countries of the world. This is called international law and it governs diplomacy, human rights, trade, and commerce, warfare, and even space travel.

International Court of Justice, The Hague, Netherlands

WHICH IS THE WORLD'S OLDEST PARLIAMENT?

Iceland has the world's oldest parliament. Called the Althing, it was founded in 930 CE by the Vikings, at Thingvellir, in southwest Iceland. The parliament operated from Thingvellir until 1798, and the original place where it stood is now a UNESCO World Heritage Site.

Site of the oldest parliament, Thingvellir, Iceland

IS A PARTICULAR DAY ELECTION DAY IN EVERY COUNTRY?

Many countries prefer to vote on Sundays. But often a country will have its own customary voting day. For example, Britain votes on Thursdays, Australia and New Zealand vote on Saturdays, while in Canada voting is held on Mondays. In the US, Tuesday is the voting day by law.

Rapid-FIRE ?

IN WHICH COUNTRY IS IT ILLEGAL NOT TO VOTE AFTER THE AGE OF 18?

Australia. If one fails to vote, it may lead to a fine and criminal charges.

Voting in Australia

IS CLIMBING TREES ILLEGAL ANYWHERE IN THE WORLD?

In Oshawa, Canada, it is against the law to climb a tree that is in the municipal area.

IN WHICH COUNTRY IS IT ILLEGAL TO CHEW GUM?

Singapore.

WHAT IS CURRENCY?

Currency is the money of a particular country. It is usually made up of paper notes and coins, and is used for buying goods or paying for services in that country. Each country has its own currency, usually issued by the government. Examples include the Japanese yen, the US dollar, the British pound, the Mongolian tugrik, or the Bhutanese ngultrum. When traveling to another country, it is necessary to obtain the money of that country.

Banknotes of different countries

WHAT WAS THE SILK ROAD?

The Silk Road was an ancient trading route. It stretched from China through Central Asia to the Mediterranean Sea. Named for the exquisite silks that China made and Europe loved to buy, the route was also used for transporting tea, spices, and many other goods.

The old Silk Road

Rapid-Fire ?

Paying by credit card

WHO MADE THE FIRST CREDIT CARD?

John Biggins, a Brooklyn banker, in 1946.

Banca Monte dei Paschi di Siena, Rome, Italy

WHICH IS THE OLDEST BANK?

Banca Monte dei Paschi di Siena, Italy, in business since 1472.

New York Stock Exchange, Wall Street, Manhattan, USA

WHICH IS THE LARGEST STOCK EXCHANGE?

The New York Stock Exchange. Shares in companies are traded at a stock exchange.

WHICH COUNTRY USED ANIMAL FUR AS CURRENCY?

Russia.

WHAT IS COUNTERFEITING?

Making and circulating fake currencies to trick people is called counterfeiting. Tampering with money is as old as money itself. Coins used to be shaved to collect precious metal, and now fake notes are printed. Various steps are taken by governments when they print money, such as adding watermarks and complicated ways of printing, to distinguish genuine notes from fake ones.

Checking whether notes are genuine

WHERE DO **PEOPLE DO BUSINESS?**

Business happens at marketplaces, shops, offices, stores, and practically anywhere where people engage in transaction. More and more business is now being conducted online.

Marketplace in Lagos, Nigeria

WHAT IS **SMUGGLING AND WHY IS IT WRONG?**

Many countries impose a tax on goods being brought into it or taken out for sale somewhere else. There may also be certain goods that are not allowed to be brought in or taken out of a country at all. Smuggling is to go against these laws and transport such goods in or out secretly—which is why it is illegal and punishable by law.

Big?

HOW HAS MONEY CHANGED OVER THE AGES?

Roman coin from the third century CE

Money is a unit of exchange used to make trade and transactions simple and flexible. It replaced the barter system in which one thing was traded for another directly—or example, exchanging a loaf of bread for some potatoes. In ancient times, all kinds of things were used as money: shells, stones, beads, even shark's teeth! Across the world, coins have been made of copper, lead, gold, and silver. Coins have been found from 5,000 years ago that were stamped to show their origin. China created the first paper money, which gradually became popular since it was light to carry. The first American currency was copper coins in 1793, and the first American paper money was used in 1862.

WHAT TYPES OF TRANSPORTATION DO PEOPLE USE?

Since the wheel was invented, humankind has progressed through newer and smarter means of transportation. Today, huge ships, modern cars, electric trains, airplanes, buses, underground trains, and other kinds of transportation take millions of people from one place to another. People have traveled beneath the surface of the ocean in submarines, and explored space using rockets and spaceships.

Underground station and train, London, UK

HOW CAN YOU
TRAVEL BENEATH THE ALPS?

Tunnels for rail and road have been built under the Alps to ease travel times. The tunnels were drilled through the rocks using enormous boring machines. The 35-mile-long Gotthard Base Tunnel in the Alps, connecting the Swiss cities of Erstfeld and Bodio, is the world's longest train tunnel.

Rapid-Fire ?

Cruise ship

WHAT IS THE DIFFERENCE BETWEEN OCEAN LINERS AND CRUISE SHIPS?

The first is used to transport people and goods from one place to another, while the second is used for pleasure trips.

Concorde

HAS ANY AIRPLANE TRAVELED AT TWICE THE SPEED OF SOUND?

Yes, Concorde. It flew between 1976 and 2003 and took three and a half hours to fly from London to New York.

Road train

WHERE ARE THE LONGEST TRUCKS?

In Australia, where there are giant trailers called "road trains."

WHAT IS THE WORLD'S BIGGEST PASSENGER JET?

The Airbus A380. This four-engined jumbo can carry up to 800 passengers! Its modern technology allows it to leave the runway quickly after landing, and also reduces the emission of greenhouse gases. It is very expensive to fly, and new Airbus A380 aircraft are no longer being built.

Airbus A380

WHERE CAN SOMEONE CATCH THE "TRAIN TO THE CLOUDS"?

The Tren a las Nubes, or "Train to the Clouds," leaves from Salta, Argentina, and reaches the Puna plateau in the Andes, after traveling up to 13,800 ft above sea level, over the highest viaduct in the world. There are oxygen tanks on board in case the altitude makes you feel sick.

The highest viaduct

WHERE ARE BOATS USED AS BUSES?

In Venice, Italy, water taxis, or water buses, called *vaporetti* are used as a means of public transportation. A *vaporetto* has a scheduled time and stops with defined routes, so passengers can use them to travel from one part of the city to another.

***Vaporetto*, Venice, Italy**

Big? WHICH IS THE LONGEST ROAD IN THE WORLD?

Pan-American Highway through the Nazca Desert, Peru

The Pan-American Highway is a network of highways, 18,640 miles long, connecting North America and South America. It passes through 14 countries that have very different climates and landscapes, including jungles, deserts, and mountains.

ARE ALL HOMES MADE THE SAME WAY?

Homes are places people build to take shelter from heat and cold, rain and snow, storms and floods. People build different kinds of homes depending on the weather and conditions they have to be protected from. The construction of their homes also depends on the kinds of materials that are readily available in an area.

WHAT ARE HOUSES LIKE IN THE ARCTIC?

In the Arctic, people need protection from extreme cold and strong storms. The Inuit use a unique traditional method of building igloos using blocks of snow. Readily available, the compressed snow traps heat and is a great insulator. Igloos are mostly temporary shelters for hunters.

Igloo

Big? WHAT ARE HOMES MADE FROM?

Humans have developed the skill of building homes from a huge variety of materials. Houses can be made of mud, stone, slate, boulders, bricks, branches, reeds, steel girders, sheets of iron, concrete, glass, wood, straw, turf, ice, bamboo, animal hides, and much more. Depending on the materials, homes differ in size, height, durability, and comfort. It can take years to build a home, but it's also possible to make one in 48 hours using 3D print technology!

Medieval stone castle, Luxembourg

WHY ARE HOUSES BUILT ON STILTS?

In places that are frequently flooded, houses are raised on stilts. This method allows homes to be constructed near water and even over lakes. At times stilts are also used to raise houses away from damaging animals and other pests. From Myanmar to Germany and Chile, houses on stilts can be found worldwide.

House on stilts, Panama

Modern home constructed of concrete

WHERE DO PEOPLE MAKE REED HOMES?

In the marshes of southern Iraq. The homes are called *mudhifs*.

***Mudhif* home**

WHAT ARE CHALETS?

Chalets are mountain homes made of wood. They have very wide, sloping roofs to handle the weight of the snow that falls, and large overhanging eaves to offer shelter. Originally found in Switzerland and the Alpine region of Europe, chalets were designed as herders' huts.

Chalet in winter

WHERE ARE *HANOK* HOUSES FOUND?

They are the traditional houses of Korea.

***Hanok* house**

DO PEOPLE LIVE UNDERGROUND?

Yes, in Coober Pedy in Australia. It is extremely hot in summer and intensely cold in winter there, but the buildings underground maintain a constant temperature of 73 °F! Miners digging for opal have used the underground spaces left behind after mining (called dugouts) to make rock houses, and even a church.

Underground home

WHO LIVES IN YURTS?

The nomads of Central Asia.

Yurt

DO PEOPLE LIVE IN TENTS?

A tent is a shelter made from fabric or material, supported by poles and secured by ropes and pegs. Traditionally, tents have been used by people seeking temporary shelters. Aboriginal people have lived in cone-shaped tents, and tents have been used by soldiers over the centuries.

Yurt in western Mongolia

Big? WHO BUILT THE FIRST SKYSCRAPERS?

Chicago skyline

Skyscrapers are tall multistory buildings that were first built in the 1880s in the USA. In the 19th century, as commercial activities grew, architects planned to accommodate the maximum number of people in a small area by extending buildings vertically rather than by spreading cities outward. Early skyscrapers reached around nine stories high, supported on an iron frame. With newer technologies, such as concrete structures, the buildings grew taller and taller. In addition to housing offices, many skyscrapers contain luxurious homes too.

WHERE DO PEOPLE LIVE IN FAIRY CHIMNEYS?

In Cappadocia, in central Turkey, volcanic eruptions have created a fascinating landscape. The leftover ash, called *tuff*, hardened and wore down into tall pillars with mushroom-shaped caps that looked like chimneys—a process that took millions of years. The local people learned to chisel the soft tuff and build homes and churches in these "chimneys."

Fairy chimneys, Cappadocia, Turkey

WHO **LIVES IN CARAVANS?**

Traditional caravans are horse-drawn wagons. The Roma people, who live mostly in Europe, live a nomadic life, moving from one campsite to another. Many, however, now inhabit more permanent camps and sometimes houses.

A vardo, a Romany wagon

WHERE IS THE **BLUE CITY?**

A street in Jodhpur

In India, the city of Jodhpur is known as the "Blue City." Most of the houses in the old town are painted blue because the people believe that blue reflects heat and keeps their homes cool. Also, the paint, which is a mixture of copper sulfate, and limestone, helps keep termites and other bugs away.

WHAT IS SPECIAL ABOUT DJENNÉ?

The spectacular city of Djenné, Mali, dating back to the 14th century, has a palace, granary, mosque, and 2,000 houses built from mud. Mud masons used mud bricks to build these magnificent homes. They are on hills to protect them from floods.

Great Mosque, Djenné, Mali

*Rapid-*FIRE **?**

CAN **HOUSES BE MADE OF BOTTLES?**

There is one made of glass bottles in British Columbia, Canada.

The Glass House, Canada

HOW **TALL IS THE WORLD'S TALLEST SKYSCRAPER?**

The Burj Khalifa in Dubai is 2,716 ft tall—two and a half times taller than the Eiffel Tower in Paris!

Burj Khalifa, Dubai

WHAT IS **UNIQUE IN MATMATA, TUNISIA?**

Cave homes made of sandstone.

Cave home

WHAT ARE **GEODESIC HOMES?**

Homes that are dome shaped.

Geodesic dome